BULLYING IS NOT JUST A KIDS' PROBLEM

It's a Matter of Civil Rights

By S. Floyd Mori

Bullying Is Not Just a Kids' Problem
It's a Matter of Civil Rights

Cover photo of the United States Capitol taken by S. Floyd Mori

**Dedicated to Anyone
Who Has Ever Been Bullied**

ACKNOWLEDGMENT

Thank you to those who have stood up to bullies and tried to make the world a better place for all.

About the Author

S. Floyd Mori is an American of Japanese heritage. He was born and raised in Utah. After graduating from high school, he joined the United States Army Reserves. He received a Bachelors and a Masters Degree from Brigham Young University with emphasis on Economics, Asian Studies, and Political Science.

He has been the National Executive Director/CEO of the Japanese American Citizens League (JACL), the oldest and largest Asian American civil and human rights organization in the United States. He was also President and Vice President on the National Board of the JACL. A major focus of the JACL is civil rights.

Previously, he taught Economics at Chabot College in Hayward, California, for ten years and served in the California State Assembly for six years. He was Mayor and City Councilman of the City of Pleasanton, California, in the 1970's. He has been a Businessman and an International Business Consultant.

He is currently President/CEO of the Asian Pacific American Institute for Congressional Studies (APAICS) in Washington, D.C. APAICS is a national non-partisan, non-profit organization dedicated to promoting Asian Pacific American participation and representation at all levels of the political process from community service to elective office. The major programs of APAICS focus on developing leadership, building public policy knowledge, and filling the political pipeline for Asian Pacific Americans to pursue public office at the local, state, and federal levels.

He has spoken and written extensively about civil rights and the Japanese American experience of World War II when 120,000 persons of Japanese ethnicity were forcibly removed from their West Coast homes and incarcerated in camps in remote and desolate areas of the country. Because he was living in Utah as a small child, he did not personally experience the incarceration. He has studied the issue and has written about that period of history and about subsequent happenings within the Asian American community. Some of his work has been published in a book entitled, *The Japanese American Story As Told Through a Collection of Speeches and Articles.*

CONTENTS

INTRODUCTION

When I grew up as virtually the only ethnic minority (except for the rest of my family) in a small farming community decades ago, not many people were concerned with the term, bullying. As a young child, I do not remember bullying as being a problem. Of course, I experienced a bit of name calling and being picked on by some of the bigger kids in the neighborhood. They made fun of me on occasion for my appearance, which was decidedly different than theirs, or for other reasons. I was sometimes excluded from activities. It was a form of bullying, but it did not cause big problems for me as I was growing up.

By today's standards, I see that I was being bullied as a child but did not realize it. Children sometimes accept the fact that life is not easy and there will be problems along the way without knowing that they are actually being bullied when they are made fun of and called derogatory names or, unfortunately in some cases, physically beaten up through no fault of their own.

Because I was the seventh of eight children with a wide spread between the oldest and the youngest, my older siblings paved the way for me. They likely endured more of the bullying and harassment, which were prevalent during World War II against people of Japanese heritage, than did I. They probably shielded me from some of the pain and hardship of that period of time.

When I was in elementary school, there were two sisters in my class who were discovered to have lice. Although we now know that anyone can get lice, in those days lice was considered as a negative issue that only faced poor people living in poverty and squalor. Those girls were tormented and ridiculed for a long time until they finally moved out of the community. In retrospect, I see that they were being treated with the cruel acts of bullying. They could not help what a life of poverty held for them. They were innocent of any wrong doing and were not to blame for their problems. Yet other children were mean to them.

People are bullied for different reasons, and bullying comes in different forms. Bullies can come in a variety of types as well. Being bullied is no fun and can cause great harm, often long lasting and sometimes permanent.

Bullying is described as aggressive behavior which is unwanted and unwarranted. The mistreatment is repeated or may be ongoing. Bullying involves actions such as name calling, threats, rumors, physical or verbal attacks, and excluding people or making fun of them. People who are bullies intimidate through belittlement for a variety of reasons. They make life miserable for others. There are also many other forms of bullying with which people are confronted as they go about their daily lives.

Bills are written, debated, and voted on within the sacred walls of the United States Capitol Building in Washington, D.C. and throughout State Capitols across the land. Most of these bills, which become laws, are enacted to ensure the safety and civil rights of citizens and other residents of this great country. People need to adhere to the laws, and the laws need to be enforced. Bullying often involves breaking laws and can lead to worse actions.

When meeting with and talking to people who have been bullied or are concerned with someone else who is being bullied, it becomes quite evident that bullying is a matter that must be addressed at every level of government and within all communities. It is an ongoing problem and concern that affects much of the general public. Too many people are suffering at the hands of bullies who have little regard for other humans. People should not have to worry about having to endure the senseless and uncalled for acts of bullying in their daily lives.

The specific cases of bullying which are included in this book are public knowledge with information about them readily available on the Internet. There are many unfortunate cases of bullying which have been documented on the Internet and through media coverage. Numerous more have not been reported or recorded.

The problem of bullying has become a huge issue for society. It is something that needs to be dealt with immediately, effectively, and continually. Bullying infringes on the civil rights of citizens and other residents.

Chapter 1

Bullying Can Affect Anyone

The majority of people in the world are basically decent, law-abiding individuals. They are not out to hurt people and make life uncomfortable and unpleasant for others. They live their lives quietly without bothering the people around them. However, there are likely to always be some who will resort to bullying others who may be weaker and more vulnerable. There is also the matter of hate, which comes into the equation. Even good people express hatred for things and people they do not like or understand. This can come across as bullying.

Bullying is not just a kids' problem. Although bullying is often considered to be a problem that mainly affects young children and teenagers, it actually has no bounds as far as age is concerned. People who are bullied can be of any age and background. However, the most vulnerable seem to be those who are smaller in stature or are overweight, may be an immigrant or of a minority ethnicity, have a physical or mental handicap, be of a lower social or economic realm, or in some way appear to be thought of as being different or inferior from what some consider the norm.

It is a fact that bullying has become a major problem of nearly epidemic proportions in some areas of the United States and perhaps even the world as people are harassed and ridiculed by others usually for small and insignificant reasons through no fault of their own. It has become a big issue in most schools and communities. There is no logical excuse for bullying, which is often a result of prejudice and discrimination.

When people are bullied, they lose their freedom and sometimes are stripped of their civil rights. Everyone should have free agency to make his or her own choices as far as the law allows. Life should not be restricted because of bullies who control where people can go, how they are supposed to act, and what they can do and say in their daily lives. Freedom should not be curtailed because of a bully who has no regard for others.

Bullies try to control vulnerable people and make their lives miserable. They ridicule and harass others so that the victims are not able to enjoy the freedoms they should have. They take away the ability, for those being bullied, to move and speak freely.

People bully others primarily for the reason to make themselves look better or to punish another individual. If they can make someone else seem less of a person, it may make them feel like they are something or someone they are not. Some people get a strange pleasure out of hurting innocent people.

Nice people do not bully others. The bullies may be mean, have low self-esteem, and could be trying to make themselves look strong and powerful in the eyes of their friends. They also could think of themselves as being superior. They pick on innocent people, smaller or different, in order to build themselves up. They generally would not bother a person who is definitely and obviously larger in stature and importance than they are. They usually avoid people who exert a high degree of self-confidence, poise, and assurance. Bullying is basically perpetrated by mean and nasty people who have little or no respect for the feelings and rights of their fellow human beings.

Many people say that they have been bullied, mainly when they were children. There are probably few people who will admit that they were a bully in their younger years. Bullying always hurts someone. It is not a pleasant or fun thing to endure. Too often bullying is taken to extremes, and the person being bullied is unable to take the abuse any longer. It is tragic when it ends in suicide, which happens all too frequently with children and young adults who have had to suffer through bullying.

There can be many unfortunate consequences from being bullied. People will feel a loss of self-esteem through constant ridicule and unkindness exhibited toward them. They may begin to suffer from emotional and physical problems as a result of the mistreatment. The emotional pain and suffering could cause the ultimate, final act of suicide when someone can take the abusive behavior of the bully or bullies no longer. It could cause death in other ways as well, possibly accidental when the bullying is taken too far and a perceived joke backfires.

Although the type of bullying for which the public seems to be currently most aware and concerned is against children in the nation's schools, it is not just a problem among kids. Older teenagers and adults, young and old, are also being bullied and belittled by some unscrupulous and rude bullies.

People who have low self-esteem and have personal problems are often thought to become the likely victims of bullies at a higher rate. That may be true, but bullying is not restricted to only those who might be considered loners or different. Popular kids can also become the victims. It may be at the hands of someone who feels jealous and envious so it seems justified to tear the other person down. Maybe the victims of bullying received a better grade or won an election so they become the object of some type of revenge for doing well. It could be that someone bullies that type of person because they think successful people are too puffed up and full of themselves. Confident people may inadvertently exude an air of superiority, which could cause others to want to punish them for their success and accomplishment. Bullies are not only targeting the desperate and lonely. Anyone can become a victim.

It is pathetic when someone running for a high political office resorts to bullying others because they are different. It is uncalled for and totally disrespectful of other humans. People running for elective office to represent the public and people who already hold elective office should be examples of respect and consideration instead of trying to make bullying acceptable by the negative things they say against innocent people.

If law enforcement officers resort to bullying innocent citizens simply for how they look or appear, that should not be acceptable. Some are being held accountable for those types of actions, but it is a big problem for certain segments of the population. It is being addressed to some degree, but it continues to be a concern causing worry and apprehension.

Bullying is an issue that needs to be addressed, and many are trying to correct the problems. It contributes to higher rates of substance abuse, depression, and suicide particularly among youth. Bullying could be curtailed more effectively with additional education, training, and good examples by those in leadership positions.

When young children and teenagers are being bullied in their neighborhoods and schools, the parents and teachers sometimes have no idea what is going on with the children. They may think the kids are just being kids with the normal everyday problems that children face in their lives. Parents may notice that there are difficulties, but they do not know the reason for them or do not consider them to be serious. They may take no action because they think the children are dealing with the problem even when they are not. Children may be holding secrets inside which are eating away at them.

Communication or a lack of it is a factor in why children do not tell adults about being bullied. Children need to feel that open communication is important and encouraged. They may be afraid, but they should feel free to tell caring adults about any problems they face. Teaching children to communicate effectively will help them to feel secure in telling someone about their problems if they become victims of bullying. Parents and teachers should help children feel confident and safe in talking to others.

Boosting the self-respect and self-esteem of children is absolutely beneficial. Children should be praised for their accomplishments and encouraged in their worthy pursuits. They should be taught to be compassionate and caring. If children are confident and feel good about themselves, they are less likely to become bullied or are able to handle it better if they are.

Families should cultivate an atmosphere in the home where everyone feels safe and secure. Home should be their haven. Bullying should not be allowed within the family confines. Bullying behavior such as relentless belittling and mercilessly teasing their siblings should be discouraged and corrected. While even the best of families will have their share of disagreements, arguments, and even fighting, these acts should not become bullying, which can cause pain and possibly violence. Siblings and parents do not always get along and arguments will occur, but bullying behavior is destructive and must be stopped in order to provide a place of peace and safety.

Bullying can be talked about regularly in the home. A plan of action could be developed in case the children are ever bullied so they will be prepared and know what to do. This should definitely include making the parents aware of the situation if and when it occurs. The children must understand that it is not their fault if they are being bullied. They need to know that there are adults who are interested in their welfare and willing to listen to them. They can find assistance with their problems. They can also be taught how to react and help others if they see bullying occurring.

13

Children do not tell others about the trials they are encountering with bullying sometimes because they are afraid of retaliation. The bully might have threatened the child who could have been told that he should expect to suffer worse consequences if he tells anyone about it. Children need to be taught that they definitely should and must tell someone if they have problems and concerns. It is too difficult a situation for them to face alone by keeping things secretly bottled up inside.

It is a rather sad fact of life that bullying can affect anyone of any age. The proper education and help from caring parents, teachers, friends, and associates can prevent people from being bullied and from becoming bullies. It will take continuous effort, but it must be done for the betterment of society.

The bully needs help, and telling an authority figure could provide the guidance needed so that the bullying behavior is put to a stop. If bullying is not curtailed among children and young people, it can cause the bullies to become more aggressive, mean, and violent. This could result in committing worse crimes against society, which may cause them to be incarcerated in a jail or prison. They will find that those places are not where they would choose to be. Bullying must be eliminated or controlled, and bullies should be made to pay for their transgressions before they resort to worse types of behavior. Many hardened criminals quite likely started out as bullies when they were much younger. Crimes of varying types involve bullying behavior and activities.

It is a good practice to be vigilant in guarding against bullying actions and deeds. If it seems evident that someone is planning to bully another person, it should be blocked and prevented if possible. Getting into physical confrontations or altercations, however, is not a good idea. It is better to seek help from responsible parties in order to avoid or stop the bullying behavior, hopefully before it starts or gets to a dangerous stage.

Although bullying is a huge problem, it can be remedied and fixed at least to a degree where it does not remain the horrible blemish on society that it is today. There will always be mean and rude people who may resort to bullying, but it should not be acceptable behavior in a civilized society where civil rights are important and valued.

Chapter 2

The Importance Of Civil Rights And Freedom

Freedom is an important and valuable thing to have in life. Free agency and having the freedom to choose what one will do or say and how to act are facts of life that most people take for granted. Bullying can take away freedom. It is a matter of civil rights, which should allow all people to enjoy freedom.

The basic concept of freedom, liberty, and free agency is the state of moving freely through society without being confined and restrained. Freedom means having the power to determine one's own actions with independence of thought. Personal liberty and freedom mean not being held under bondage or slavery. Freedom is important to our way of life, and there is great value in having freedom as part of everyday living.

Most Americans enjoy freedom and liberty without giving it much thought. Freedom is expected and enjoyed. It is something which is generally considered as a right and privilege. People and nations in the free world are sacrificing to try and bring freedom and democracy to other nations where people are suffering from oppression and a lack of freedom.

The Founding Fathers of the United States of America decided how the country would function as a free nation. They wrote these words in the second paragraph of the Declaration of Independence, "We hold these truths to be self-evident, that all men are created equal, that they are endowed by their Creator with certain unalienable Rights, that among these are Life, Liberty, and the Pursuit of Happiness. That to secure these rights, Governments are instituted among Men, deriving their just powers from the consent of the governed."

Freedom may mean different things to different people, but there are some common threads throughout the word and concept. Freedom is having free agency or the right to choose what a person will say and do without having to worry about it. People in a free society have equal rights as much as possible. There are laws enacted which may restrict some of the freedom, but basic freedoms remain intact for all people as long as they adhere to certain regulations and do not break laws. They should not act in a manner that takes away the freedom of others.

Free people have the legal right to do whatever they want as long as they are obeying the laws and not bringing harm to another person or coercing others to do unlawful or harmful practices. Freedom generally includes protecting oneself and watching out for your own welfare as much as possible.

People must learn self-control and compassion for others while dealing in a free society. It is not allowed to infringe on other people's freedom at the peril of their health and well being. Although people who are free are empowered to take care of themselves, there are limitations.

When people become bullies and bother people to the extent of harassment and danger to the other person, they take away the freedom of people who are most likely innocent persons. Bullies have no regard for the welfare of others. They are thinking only of trying to benefit themselves or to gain some gratification or personal enjoyment from harming others.

Bullies take away people's freedom by making it impossible for them to move and act freely as they would like. Victims of bullying feel intimidated and restrained. They are not able to enjoy the freedom to achieve and succeed or even to move freely if they are being harassed at every turn. Those being bullied may actually be held in a type of bondage if some bully has control over them and is restricting their actions.

Verbal and physical attacks against totally innocent people can be made for no logical reason. When people are faced with violence or coercion by another person who is trying to intimidate them, it is a type of bullying. It takes away their free agency. Bullies most certainly do violate the freedom of others.

While freedom does include the basic freedom of speech and bullies are free to say what they wish to an extent, it should not be used to curtail the freedom and well being of others. People should be able to act according to their own desires in most cases, but it should not harm and destroy other people. The laws and common sense must be observed.

Racial epithets are not to be allowed as they demean and diminish an innocent person simply for their ethnicity. It may be an

16

unwritten law to which the public should adhere to respect the rights of others by not resorting to name calling of a degrading nature.

Civil rights have been a big issue in government as laws are made and enacted. This is an important aspect of freedom so that people are created equally without bias and prejudice. A history of repression and discrimination needs to be addressed continually so that people are able to live freely without fear. Although great strides have been made in some areas of civil rights, there are other areas where not a lot has changed over decades of hard work and effort to rectify the disparaging matters.

There have been periods in the history of the United States when the Constitution did not protect innocent persons who were incarcerated through no fault of their own. People have been treated poorly and persecuted simply for their ethnicity because of the prejudice of others. Political leaders and law enforcement personnel are relied upon to enforce the law and take care of bullying problems if and when they reach their sphere of influence.

Freedom and civil rights are valuable aspects of life and must be maintained for the growth and progression of people as they pursue their dreams. Bullies should not be allowed to steal those dreams and ruin anyone's future.

Chapter 3

Types And Consequences Of Bullying

Normally, we think of bullying as some big kids picking on smaller children by pushing them around or calling them names and saying unkind things to them. That might be the most common type of bullying, but it is not the only kind. Bullying takes many shapes and forms.

There was a childhood saying which went like this: "Sticks and stones may break my bones, but names will never hurt me." Children would say it to each other. These words were expressed by parents and elementary school teachers to show children that they should accept the fact that people would not always be nice and that they might be called names. The children were told that name calling could be tolerated because the words did not cause physical harm such as stones could. That practice of name calling has come to be known as verbal abuse. It should not be acceptable just as physically beating up a person should not be tolerated. Words can and indeed DO hurt. Those are forms of bullying which should not occur, but they still exist.

Although there are cases of people being bullied and hurt such as by fighting and hitting by bullies and gang members, it seems that the majority of bullying cases are verbal abuse and taunts, which can also be very damaging. Most people do not have a thick skin, and words can hurt perhaps as deeply as physical abuse.

Saying unkind things either publicly or privately about a person's ethnicity, appearance, weight, handicap, speech, clothing, living conditions, or anything else over which the person being bullied has no control can be extremely hurtful and cause great pain. Intimidating someone through negative words and actions can do permanent damage.

Bullies are mean and scary. They can use tactics that cause physical pain, but more often the bullying entails taunts and verbal threats. This can create problems for the entire being, emotionally, mentally, and physically.

Bullies are rude and annoying people who normally have little respect for themselves and certainly not for those to whom they direct their bullying. Their actions hurt and destroy others who are sometimes innocent bystanders who certainly do not deserve such mistreatment. Whispering and talking about people behind their back or even to their face by telling untruths or rumors about them is also a form of bullying. Although it can happen that bullies torment their friends, they usually direct their bullying to people that they do not know or just know slightly.

Racial slurs are a common form of bullying. Just because someone looks or acts different is no reason for them to be the object of bullying and being persecuted with racial epithets. Unfortunately, people are still doing this even though conditions have been markedly improved since the challenging of civil rights violations started decades ago. No one likes to be called names, and name calling hurts. People who do this type of behavior are showing themselves to be extremely crude and unkind. Ignorant people continue to use those terms of belittlement toward people of different ethnicities even though it is considered as absolutely unacceptable in today's society. It remains a problem among young and old.

Immigrants are sometimes bullied and ridiculed for the way they speak or the way they look and dress. Physical characteristics with which a person is born are not something over which most people can have control. Language may be a reason for ridicule if a person does not have command of the English language. People who study foreign languages realize that learning a language can be very difficult and time consuming. Many immigrants do not have the time and means to study and learn the English language well. They may feel that they have more important things to do such as earning a living.

Religion should not be a cause for bullying. People have religious freedom to worship as they please. History has shown many cases of religious intolerance against various sects. People should be free to practice their religion freely. If that involves certain forms of dress, it should not be a reason to ridicule and bully.

Since the horrible tragedy of 9-11, American Muslims and others are being routinely bullied and disrespected for no reason other than their appearance and the prejudice of certain people. They may have similar appearances to some of the terrorists. Mean and intolerant people are persecuting them for no reason other than wrong perceptions and hate. Innocent children are being bullied in schools simply for how they look even though they are American citizens who have no ties to any terrorists. Unwarranted violence against them has increased.

Racial profiling is something, which is discouraged by most and encouraged by some political leaders and ordinary citizens. People are profiled simply for how they look. This happened to innocent Japanese Americans during World War II when almost the entire population of Americans of Japanese heritage born in the United States but living on the West Coast were incarcerated. The injustice of the mass incarceration, which was facilitated by unjust racial profiling, should never be allowed to happen again to anyone else.

Even though the lifestyle and civil rights actions of the recent past include gay people finding increased acceptance in the world today, bullying against them is still prevalent. Sexual orientation has long been an issue for which bullies target innocent people and harass them. It is again a matter of hate and intolerance, which causes the violent physical and verbal attacks against this segment of the population. It is uncalled for in this world where innocent people should be able to enjoy freedom and civil rights no matter who they are.

Cyber bullying is also becoming a big problem with people feeling that they can harass others without being found out. Messages are given anonymously to or against an unsuspecting victim who usually does not ever find out who is sending the messages. Posts are also done publicly to ridicule another person who has no recourse. Many people see the posts which can bring great shame and harm to the person being victimized. Although the highly skilled technical experts in law enforcement are able to detect the senders who may think they can remain anonymous, bullies may not realize that they are likely to be caught. Bullying through cyber crime is a big problem.

There are cases of parents basically bullying their children in a variety of ways. Physical and verbal abuse of children is a form of bullying which should be addressed. Not all children have loving parents, and parents often have problems that make parenting difficult for them. It is unfortunate that social workers and law enforcement must sometimes step in to help the children who are being bullied in their own homes. Parenting is not easy, but help is available. Even the best of parents may occasionally find themselves needing to seek help or to just take time out for themselves in order to prevent bullying of their children.

Caring for older or handicapped family members may be a hardship for people who are unable to cope. It may be necessary to get outside assistance before problems escalate to the point where someone resorts to bullying behavior.

People who are caregivers may need outlets to help in their own well being so that bullying does not become an issue. There are ways and means for people to receive outside support by government and private agencies as well as volunteers in matters involving caring for another person.

Bullying in all forms can cause great pain to an innocent person. Bullying is the cause of a lot of unnecessary unhappiness and depression which can result in diminishing the progress and learning of a child or adult. Mental and social ills are a result of bullying

The many types of bullying must be addressed in order to make bullying become less of a problem for society in general and individuals in particular.

Chapter 4

Combating The Problems Of Bullying

Education is the key in the fight to combat the problem of bullying. The education and training to combat bullying can take several forms and be undertaken by various groups including schools, government agencies, law enforcement, and the home.

The home is the ideal place for people to learn how to treat others. Friends and associates will come and go, but family is always family (although there may be cases of estrangement). The family members should be kind and loving to each other. The family should be the place where people can find acceptance and feel safe. The home should be a refuge against the possible pain and hardship of the outside world.

Children learn important lessons in school, but the home is the place where they generally become instilled with their value systems. Churches are also effective in helping build character and teach values.

There are many problems within families. The example of kindness and acceptance is all too often not taught in the home because of the lifestyle or prejudices of the parents and adults. Children who become bullies may be taught prejudice and discrimination from their parents. They may be told that they are superior and better than other people. They may be poor and feel that the world owes them something. Bullies might also act out against others because of the ill treatment they receive at home.

There are various ways to combat the problem of bullying. When someone is aggressively harassing and bullying another person, sometimes action should be taken but usually it is better to avoid the confrontation or walk away.

It is not easy to simply ignore the insults and remarks, or the rumors being spread, about the victim. It is better not to try and retaliate because things could escalate and become worse. The bully may begin to treat the person being bullied worse than previously.

There is safety in numbers. Bullies will often do their evil deeds only when they are not alone. They want to have people around them to defend them and support them in the ill treatment they are showering on another person. They may be showing off in front of their friends to make themselves look more powerful. Victims should also realize that having people around them is a good thing. Walking with friends and having other people around could help the people being bullied.

Avoiding the bully may be easier said than done as often bullies come upon someone at the most inopportune times without notice. Taking a different path or route than what is normal may confuse the bullies so they are not there waiting to pounce on an innocent person. Changing one's routine could help to stop the bullying or evade it.

The bully wants to get a reaction from the person he bullies. It is best to try not to respond to them or their taunting. Ignoring them is the best course of action. Walking away may help to not allow the confrontation to become worse. It is not easy to deal with bullies, but people should find ways to avoid being victims.

If someone persists in bullying to the point of destruction and hardship, another responsible person should definitely be told. Sometimes it helps to just talk with someone else about the problem. Children should tell a parent, a teacher, or another adult about the bullying. Perhaps they should tell a friend who could then report the issue to an adult. Telling another person can help the victim feel better, and people in authority should be able to help. If someone sees another person being bullied, it is best to tell someone about it. Bullying should not be allowed to escalate to the point of causing bigger problems.

Having a friend or someone close by take a video of the bullying could help to verify that it is actually happening and is a problem. In this day and age of cell phones on which video cameras are readily available, it should be easy to document what is happening. Most children own cell phones and are adept at taking videos.

Trying to be kind and civil to the bully is not easy, but it just might cause a positive reaction. It could help turn the bully around, but that may not be likely. People who are being bullied should realize that it is not their fault. They are not alone in the type of treatment they are getting. However, they should not accept the bullying tactics against them. They should seek and receive help.

When people are bullied, they may need to seek guidance and assistance from another party. Children may be afraid to tell a responsible adult such as a teacher or parent because they are afraid of retaliation or revenge. They may not want to be a snitch or to cause any trouble.

The bully needs to be confronted for his own good. It is unlikely that he could ever become a responsible adult and get through life if he does not stop being a bully. Bullies need to be held accountable for their actions. They need to realize the consequences of their behavior. If they continue to be bullies, they can ruin the future of innocent people and their own future as well.

If the bullying matter is something that is causing a dangerous situation, parents, school authorities, or even the police should become involved. Innocent people should not have to endure bullying.

People need to be empowered to take control of their own lives. Finding help from outside sources may be necessary. Otherwise, they will lose their freedom as they suffer the pains of bullying.

Chapter 5

Children Are Often Victims of Bullying

Bullying against children of elementary school and junior high school age has escalated in recent years. Children are often the innocent victims of vicious bullying. There are more incidents of harassment against people of different ethnicities such as American Muslims after the horrific actions of 9-11. Cases of bullying because of sexual orientation and religious preference are seen and documented.

There are all manner of reasons that children may find themselves victims of bullying. They may erroneously or possibly correctly be looked upon as being different, poor, not smart, or otherwise seemingly inferior in some manner.

The strides in civil right that have resulted in many laws being changed to be more inclusive of everyone have been curtailed in some respects by people bullying others. It is not clear why bullying has become such a big problem of enormous proportions. Hate fueled by discrimination and prejudice is a major factor.

Young children and teenagers are adept at using social media as their main means of communication. They seem to all know how to use the Internet, smart phones, and social networks to their advantage. These outlets potentially provide them with huge audiences. Videos they post online can become viral and reach thousands of people in a short period of time. This has made cyber bullying a major problem among children and teens.

It is true that bullying is nothing new. It has been around for decades to some degree, but it was not the huge problem in the past that it is today. Some kids were always being picked on by bullies, but the bullies didn't bother everyone. Most people who are adults now were probably not bullied as children. Now studies indicate that possibly three fourths of the teenagers studied have been bullied with much of it being online.

Even friends can have arguments and be at odds with each other. Instead of talking it out and working on the problem, they may resort to social media to make disparaging remarks and comments about the other person. They don't realize that the damage is done once it is placed online for the world to see. Although posts may be subsequently removed, some harm may already have been done. Other students might make comments to the original negative post, causing further difficulties. The friendship will likely be destroyed, and the reputation of both parties could suffer big consequences. People may also find themselves in big trouble from their actions.

The rise and seriousness of cyber bullying cannot be denied. It is widespread and destructive. People are suffering in silence and in public because of this unfortunate situation of being bullied on the Internet. It has caused too many serious consequences such as even death from suicide.

Children who suffer from and may be treated for ADHD (Attention Deficit Hyperactivity Disorder) face a risk of being bullied at school and in social settings. ADHD is a condition that is characterized by the inability to pay attention and having little control over their impulses and emotions. They may become the targets for bullies because of actions inadvertently made. Some studies have stated that children with ADHD are ten times more likely than their peers to be victims of bullying.

Any type of physical or mental ailment such as autism, which makes a child different from most of the normal school crowd, can be a reason to be bullied. There are many causes for children to act different than the norm. Other children often do not take time to get to know the child or the reasons for his behavior, but they just resort to bullying someone who is different. That is a horrible case of unkindness to bully someone with a disability or health problem.

Being poor or having a lack of financial resources can be a reason for being bullied. Physical appearance includes clothing. If a child's parents cannot afford stylish clothes that are thought to be fashionable, the child may be bullied by being made fun of in front of others. That is said to be one reason that some schools opt for school uniforms that can make the distinction between the clothes of the rich and poor less of an issue.

The matter of free food at schools has become a topic for discussion. Some are advocating for all students to receive free meals in order that there will be no distinction between those who have and those who have not. Although school officials try not to make it obvious who exactly is receiving the free meals, the children seem to know what is going on in the cafeteria. Some bullies may torment children who are from families having financial difficulties and receiving free food at schools.

Peer pressure may cause kids to bully others. They may succumb to the enticement and taunts of their friends who want them to join in the supposed fun of ridiculing another person. Even though they do not really want to participate, younger children or teenagers may do it because they want to be one of the crowd. They might think it will help them socially to be included in what they perceive to be the popular group.

Some kids want the power that they feel when they have control over someone else. The Internet gives them the feeling that they are able to influence others. They may not realize that they are doing great harm to another human being. They may consider it to be just good, clean fun. They could even be prosecuted for some of their actions if they warrant such punishment. They think they are having a good time, and they disregard the possible consequences, which could be very serious.

Many children are missing school because of bullying against them. They will fake illness to avoid facing the bullies at school. They may become reclusive and avoid other people. They could feel fear in facing someone who has been harassing them. They might be reluctant to say anything to others because they are afraid of retaliation and worse treatment against them.

Everyone wants to have friends and to be accepted. Some teenagers are desperate to be considered popular. They may do anything asked of them to feel that they are part of the "in" group. They may do bad things such as bullying to be accepted. They don't realize that people who would use those bullying tactics against others are not the kind of friends they should have or would want if they really knew their true motives and character.

There are even cases of suicide among children and young teenagers when they are bullied to the extent that they feel their only relief will be to end their life. That is a tragedy that children have to feel such desperation and loneliness that they would resort to suicide. It is a shame that parents, teachers, or friends could not step in to show the person that he or she is of great worth. Usually, however, no one suspected that the problem was that severe so no one stepped up to the plate to prevent it.

All bullies are not of the low self-esteem variety who are merely trying to buoy themselves up by their cruel behavior. They could be people who feel that they are entitled and above the norm. They may feel that they have the privilege to exert their power because they are important. They might be filled with pride in the person they think they are and look down on those who they deem to be inferior.

Various research studies have indicated that school children who are bullied are more than twice as likely to consider suicide and think about ending their lives. There are too many cases where children do actually attempt suicide with too many of them being successful in that fateful endeavor. Thoughts about killing themselves and attempted suicides are often directly linked to bullying in a significant number of cases among children and adolescents.

People are targeted by bullies for some reason although the reason may not be clear. Victims are not necessarily the type who are considered to become likely victims. All kids should be vigilant so they will not become the unwitting victims. If a bullying incident happens, it needs to be stopped immediately so that the destructive behavior does not continue. It could cause devastating results if the bullying action were to be allowed to be perpetuated over and over again.

Although many murders are the result of bullying behavior of some variety, most bullies do not actually kill their victims. However, bullies can cause others to be bullied to death. It is a tragic event when innocent young lives are shattered and snuffed out simply because someone else bullied an innocent human being.

Children who are bullied should realize that it is not their fault. The bully is responsible for his actions. He deserves to be punished and rebuked for the unkind deeds he does. He is likely to have an extremely difficult time as an adult if that destructive behavior continues.

Too many adults such as parents and teachers may have the mistaken notion that bullying is a part of living that every child will experience in some form. They may consider it as a fact of life that makes children stronger and more resilient. It is not true that bullying is harmless as it can cause much pain and suffering to those being bullied.

Chapter 6

Young Adults Are Not Immune From Bullying

It may be thought that young adults who have made it through the difficulties of the teen years and high school have now got it made. They may inaccurately be considered as no longer likely potential victims of bullying. It might seem that they are now safe from the dangers and difficulties of being bullied. It would be fortunate if that were true, but that is not always the case.

Completing and leaving high school is no guarantee that bullying will stop or not accompany a person. There are cases where older teenagers and young adults also suffer from being bullied. Sometimes people who were not bullied while they were children might suddenly find themselves as victims.

The hazing incidents which occur on college campuses, particularly with freshmen who may join a fraternity have become big news. Several young men have died after being bullied to do things they would not ordinarily do. They were forced to drink large amounts of alcohol or do dangerous acts, which proved to be injurious to their health. Unfortunately, sometimes this mistreatment of fellow students, who should be caring brothers, has resulted in the early demise of college students who could have had a good future. They were prematurely taken from this earthly life through the senseless acts of bullying.

Sports are a big part of college life. Most students either participate in various athletic endeavors or else they are spectators. Coaches who are looked up to and respected should not use bullying tactics against their players. They should not allow their team members to bully each other. Those in leadership positions have a responsibility to curtail and stop any bullying that may occur. The type of hazing that sometimes happens in fraternities seems to occur also within athletic teams.

The bullying which takes place could be athletes against non-athletes, rich against poor, smart against not so smart, popular against not so popular, or a combination of these. People make fun of others without thinking. The consequences of such behavior should be considered, and bullying should not be tolerated.

Young women are not immune from bullying tactics from each other as some cases have been reported among sororities and women's athletic teams. No one is immune from bullying and entirely safe from it.

There have been several well-publicized cases of bullying, hazing, and discrimination against college students. It is an ongoing problem, which has been going on for many years. These actions are now becoming known as especially destructive forms of bullying. Many students report that they have been bullied in some way while attending college. It is usually perpetrated by another student or other students, but the bully could be a professor or coach. Some report having seen other students being bullied by professors.

Another problem that happens with young adults all too often involves sexual violence and misconduct of one person against an innocent victim. Young women fall prey to unwanted sexual advances and possibly even rape when they are vulnerable. They should be aware of potential trouble that could arise and keep themselves out of situations, which they could regret. Staying away from alcohol use is a good practice although drinking is extremely popular among young adults and the public at large. Television shows regularly depict people, even police officers and athletes, drinking alcohol to relax after work. Drinking to excess is a bad practice for anyone, and it can have devastating results if young people particularly are not careful.

Generally, college students are making a whole new set of friends. As high school students graduate, they go their separate ways. Few attend the same college as their friends from high school. Athletes particularly usually go alone to a college where they will pursue their dreams because of possibly receiving an athletic scholarship and joining a team. The same is true for the rest of the students as they go off to various colleges across the country or world. They don't have their same set of friends, and they could become the object of bullying by people who do not know them personally or well.

Students go to college without their parents around. They are suddenly thrust into a new way of life where they are free to make their own decisions and choices. They likely will not have a lot of adult supervision in their daily lives except for limited interaction with teachers. They may be trying new things and experiencing a different way of life. They could be bullied or become bullies as they face life without the constant adult supervision, which their parents should have been providing.

Most freshmen college students who go away from home and live in dormitories are assigned a roommate. They may not know this person. They will try to get along, but difficulties could arise as they are sharing so much of their life and time together. The roommates may participate in the same sports, eat together, study together, and play together. Getting along is not always easy, and a person could become the object of bullying as a result.

Students may at times feel uncomfortable in this new lifestyle to which they must become accustomed at a young age. There is a lot of pressure for college students to do well and succeed. It may not be easy to concentrate on what they need to do. Stress may enter the equation. They may feel undue pressure which lowers their resistance to outside forces which may tear them down or cause them to do things they would not ordinarily choose to do. They could be talked into taking part in some bullying of an innocent student or they could become the object of such harassment.

Cyber bullying is also a problem for college students as they are completely computer savvy, and they absolutely know all about how to use social media and the Internet. Students are connected through Twitter, Facebook, Instagram, and other social networks, and they know how to use them for good or bad. Unfortunately, bullies are increasingly using social media.

There have been cases of college students killing themselves after someone has made derogatory comments and posts about them on social media. Those who do the bullying and post negative information usually do not mean to do any permanent harm. They may have just wanted to show themselves in a more favorable light or they thought they were just having some fun. It is extremely unfortunate when the bully and the person bullied have their lives ruined because of some post on social media.

College students who are being bullied should try to talk to someone before making the decision which will ultimately ruin their life. Everyone needs a friend, and friends can be valuable allies in combating bullying. Friends should look out for each other. If a situation looks bad, maybe a friend needs to intervene or get help from someone else such as a professor, coach, or dean. All colleges provide counseling services, which could be utilized by any victims of bullying. Disasters could be avoided with more people in tune to helping or seeking help when it is warranted.

The years of college should be fun. They should be full of learning and adventure. This is an important period of life for young people. This should be a time to make new friends and enjoy life. It should not be a time of sadness and desperation because of bullying.

Young adults who complete college and enter the workforce or who seek employment directly out of high school may also find themselves in unfamiliar territory. They are thrust into situations, which are new to them as they encounter various fellow employees and bosses with whom they must spend most waking hours. They are having new experiences with newly acquired friends and associates. They could encounter situations where they are not looked at favorably and they may become bullied. These situations require the same remedies of finding a friend and someone to talk to about the problems. It is important not to let things get to the point where they are adversely affecting the victim's life, health, and well being.

Young adults are generally fairly well grounded so that they are able to make their way in the world admirably. They need to have or develop the self-confidence to move through life effectively with its challenges and trials. No one will escape from the troubles and tribulations in life, but there is no reason to accept being bullied.

Life holds great promise for young people, and bullies should not be allowed to ruin it for them.

Chapter 7

Bullying Problems In The Military

Movies have long depicted bullying in the U.S. military. Sergeants who have command of other soldiers are usually shown calling their subordinates names and ridiculing them. They think nothing of belittling them in front of their peers. They yell at the soldiers and often swear at them after singling them out for mistreatment. The old war movies showed the officers generally as being mean and rude to the soldiers who were under their command. Hopefully, conditions regarding this issue have improved in the military as cases have come to light, which indicate a very real problem of bullying in the military.   Intimidation and bullying in the military have been around for centuries even from the early days of the Roman Empire. Officers in the Armed Forces regularly seemed to pick out certain soldiers who would be regularly yelled at in front of others. They demeaned and belittled them as a presumed means to build character and develop strength of body and spirit.

Of course, not all officers behave in a bullying manner. Many are kind and caring individuals who have great concern for those under their command. They serve with integrity. They are leaders and mentors who have great influence on young people serving in the military. The Armed Forces provide a good training ground, which builds character, but bullying should not be a part of it.

The United States military has been addressing the bullying tactics within their ranks at least since the 1990's, but the bullying continues. It is still a problem as someone who is either slightly or largely different is singled out for cruel treatment. Those who are involved with showering the person with the bullying tactics may think it is all in fun or that they are building character as the actions were thought to do in days long past. They may consider it as a rite of passage for the person. They might think it is funny to cause another person to be ridiculed and laughed at by his peers.

Private Danny Chen was bullied in the military. Danny was born on May 26, 1992, in Chinatown, Manhattan, New York City, where he was raised. He graduated from Pace University High

School in Manhattan in 2010 and received a full scholarship to Baruch College also in Manhattan, where he had taken classes the summer after high school. His father worked as a chef, and his mother was a seamstress. His parents were immigrants from China.

Danny wanted to join the U.S. Army and become a soldier. He would forgo college for the time being. He had desired to become a New York City police officer after he finished with the Army and college. Danny was an only child, and his mother did not want him to join the Army. She desired for him to attend college and to have a safe occupation like perhaps a pharmacist.

Many Chinese families would not allow their sons born in America, especially if they were the only son, to join the Army because sons are prized in their culture. The Army was considered dangerous and undesirable. Danny's wish, however, was to join the military and serve his country. He apparently thought the Army would be good training for his future police work.

On October 3, 2011, when he was nineteen years old, Private Danny Chen was found dead in Afghanistan of what the Army described as "an apparent self-inflicted gunshot wound." His parents were devastated, of course. The matter was investigated.

Later the story emerged that a group of Danny's superiors in the Army allegedly tormented him on an almost daily basis over the course of around six weeks in Afghanistan. They singled him out. He was the only Chinese American and apparently the only Asian American soldier in their unit. They hurtled racial slurs at him. They forced him to do sprints while carrying a sandbag. They ordered him to crawl along the ground while other soldiers threw rocks at him. They basically bullied him everyday seemingly simply for his ethnicity because he was different from the rest of them. It seems to have been a clear case of racial bias and prejudice by his superior officers and other soldiers.

A sergeant is said to have dragged Danny out of bed on September 27, 2011. Danny was then forced to crawl over gravel, leaving bruises and cuts on his back. Although the incident was said to have been reported to his platoon sergeant and squad leader, it was apparently not reported to their superior officers. Nothing came of the incident with no reprimands being received by the perpetrators.

On the day that Danny died, other soldiers had forced him to crawl on gravel over 300 feet while carrying Army equipment as fellow soldiers threw rocks at him. They were likely laughing at him. Apparently, it was more than he could take as he was found dead not long after that experience. It was certainly not the first time he had been subjected to such cruel mistreatment. He received a military funeral at a cemetery in Valhalla, New York, on October 13, 2011.

This was an extreme case of racial tensions and bullying. People who thought they were better than Danny seemingly because he was of Asian descent and the son of immigrants treated him poorly. They obviously did not like him for some reason. Diversity is a fact of life and needs to be understood and encouraged. Intolerance and racism are still big problems in the military and elsewhere in American society.

Danny was not the type who would be expected to be bullied. He was tall at 6'4", but he was thin. Perhaps his personality offended the officers, but it seems to have been mainly a racial issue. He was persecuted and mistreated simply for his ethnicity and who he was. The harassment and bullying took its toll. He could take it no longer so he opted for suicide.

Unfortunately, he was not able to ignore the treatment and walk away. His situation was such that he could not avoid the bullies. They were constantly around him and making his life miserable each day. His perceived experience of what the Army would be like as he had wanted to serve his country became a nightmare.

The U.S. Army had not taught these soldiers about diversity and inclusion or even kindness for that matter. They exhibited their prejudice and racism on an innocent young soldier. There were eight defendants in the case. They faced various charges, including involuntary manslaughter, assault, dereliction of duty, making false statements, negligent homicide, and reckless endangerment. After a series of hearings, the most serious charge of involuntary manslaughter was dropped. Four of the soldiers were recommended for court martial on the remaining charges which could carry a three year prison sentence. Subsequent trials were held at Fort Bragg in North Carolina, and some of the charges were dropped.

The result of these totally senseless and brutal acts of bullying was the loss of life of a fine young man. Another unfortunate consequence of the actions of those soldiers who did the bullying was that they ruined their own lives as well as Danny's. They were dishonored with some receiving a court martial. Their careers and reputations were ruined. Although their names may not be remembered, they have the terrible blemish on their record and they have to live with what they did. They basically caused the death of a fellow soldier. That may not have been their intent, but that was the outcome of their actions. Bullying is never a good idea.

Another young Chinese American member of the military was a twenty-one year old U.S. Marine from California named Harry Lew. It was April in 2011 when he was experiencing severe punishment and bullying from his fellow Marines. The Marines were angry at Lew because he fell asleep during guard duty, which was considered a serious crime in the military. It happened more than once. Instead of checking to see if there were physical reasons for his falling asleep on duty, his fellow Marines bullied and brutalized him. They demanded that Lew perform physical tasks, and they would stomp on his back and legs if he failed to do an exercise correctly. Sand was poured on Lew's chest and face as he lay on his back.

A fellow Marine punched Lew in the back of the head so hard that his attacker's knuckles were cut in the process. Less than an hour after that incident, Lew would be dead. The punch did not kill him, but he apparently committed suicide with his own machine gun. Lew wrote on his arm, before taking his own life, "may hate me now, but in the long run this was the right choice I'm sorry my mom deserves the truth."

Lew was the nephew of Congresswoman Judy Chu from California. Congresswoman Chu told the story to members of Congress about her nephew, who she said was looking forward to returning home after three months longer in the service of his country. The Congresswoman has become an advocate for enforcing the rules against hazing in the military. The bullying tactics used against Lew by his fellow Marines undoubtedly caused him to resort to suicide. His final act brought the issue to the forefront by his unfortunate death. This may have been his motivation to help others who could have been suffering from bullying by their fellow servicemen or officers.

These two cases of bullying in the military were both apparently motivated by racial issues such as prejudice and discrimination. They happened in two separate branches of the military, but both were against young Americans of Chinese heritage. Of course, all ethnic minority men and women in the military are not bullied, and there are many reasons other than racism for people to be bullied. People could be treated in that manner in the military because of gender issues and sexual orientation. The bully may just take a disliking to the person and let it show through bullying.

Unfortunately, the cases of Danny Chen and Harry Lew are just two of many cases of bullying in the military. Most do not result in such a tragic and final outcome. These cases illustrate a problem, but Asian Americans are not the only people bullied in the military. Others of ethnically diverse backgrounds and women have been harassed and bullied while in the service of their country in the Armed Forces. Although racial issues continue to be a problem because of continuing prejudice, there are other reasons for bullying as well such as being different in another way. Bullying is being addressed by the military, but it remains a major issue.

All branches of the service have had cases reported of bullying abuse by officers and fellow soldiers. It remains a problem, and it causes much hardship for young people serving our country.

The rate of suicide in the military has increased in the last decade with the wars in Iraq and Afghanistan. Pressures are immense for military personnel, but bullying should not be tolerated and should not be the reason for the suicides. The people who are being bullied need to know that seeking help is not a sign of weakness. Bullying should be reported to superiors. People should look out for and help each other. When they see bullying and harassment, they should not hesitate to report them.

The modern military of the United States and most free countries is a more professional military, and such bullying tactics as were used and accepted freely in the past should not be allowed. Continued education in this area must be ongoing and mandatory to be effective.

Chapter 8

Bullying Affects Older People As Well

As previously stated, generally we think of bullying as a problem among young children and teenagers, but it can happen to anyone. This includes young adults, middle-aged people, and senior citizens. People can be cruel at any age, and older people are also becoming victims of bullies.

There have been cases on subway trains and on buses where teenagers have harassed an older person. A group of teenagers may crowd around a lone passenger who is older. They may taunt and ridicule him while he is innocently riding public transit. That is a totally uncalled for type of bullying. It is entirely random and cruel. The victim is generally not able to do anything to defend himself as he is outnumbered. He actually should do nothing to provoke the bullies further, but he should ignore them and get away from them as soon as possible. The incident should also be reported to the authorities although it is unlikely that the perpetrators will be apprehended.

It is quite likely that most people enjoy their work and do not have problems of bullying in the workplace. However, people are sometimes bullied in their office or place of business by their boss or coworkers. There is likely more bullying in the workplace than anyone knows or admits. A supervisor might be bullying one or more of the employees under him. A co-worker may be bullying another worker. Various projects, promotions, locations, and conditions in the workplace may cause people to be bullied or to bully others. This can be very destructive to the morale of the staff and damaging to the person being bullied. It can ruin the health and well being of the person being bullied. This can happen to people of any age, young or old.

One of the most well known cases of an older adult being bullied is the school bus monitor in New York, which happened in 2012. It was June so school must have been nearly over for the year. This sixty-nine year old woman had been a school bus driver for twenty years. She spent three years as a school bus monitor, simply riding the bus to try and help students behave themselves while on the bus. She was not unfamiliar with working with young students. She was simply doing her job when the bullies confronted her. It may have been going on for many days or months.

Four boys were taunting and bullying her. She was apparently being ridiculed, sworn at, and threatened by this group of seventh graders. Her appearance and weight were criticized. The cruelty of these four adolescent boys was thoughtless, rude, and horribly unkind.

The boys told her that she did not have a family because they all killed themselves because they did not want to be near her. She had actually had a son who committed suicide a decade earlier. It must have hurt badly to be hurtled with such harsh and heartless comments about her family.

It would not have been the first time that the woman had to endure the ridicule and harassment from the young students, but this time a fellow student on the bus recorded it on his cell phone. After posting the video and having it go viral, it reached 1.4 million views. The woman who had been bullied did not know that the video was being made. The student may have been trying to help her or he may have been simply having some fun at her expense. She can be grateful to the student who made the video because it totally changed her life.

When a young man in Canada heard about the situation, he set up an online collection for her intending to raise a little money to give her a vacation. Little could he know that it would receive the response that it did. More than 32,000 people in 84 countries pledged more than $700,000 in donations. She was able to quit her job on the school bus and did not have to deal with the bullying and cruelty any longer. She was given a life changing amount of money through the efforts and kindness of strangers.

She used $100,000 of that money as seed money to start an anti-bullying foundation promoting a message of kindness. She now travels to promote her foundation and participate in anti-bullying events. She has used her unfortunate experience of being the victim of bullies to help others.

There was one of the four boys who were involved in the bullying incident who came to her home with his parents to apologize. The other three sent written apologies. They may have been forced to do it, and the woman does not believe they were sincere. The experience was also undoubtedly life changing for them as well since it has branded them as bullies. Their names may not be known, but people close to them would know who they are. It is something they will have to endure throughout their lives.

Her advice to others is that unless you have something nice to say, don't say anything at all. She has found that there are lots of good people out there and that you must ignore the negative and bad people who try to hurt you.

A method of bullying targeting senior citizens is regarding working from home. Many seniors are having a hard time financially and are looking for ways to supplement the meager income they have through social security, pensions, or other means. They may be looking for some online opportunity to earn just a little extra money. There are scams by the hundreds or thousands being perpetrated by dishonest persons who are trying to trick or bully senior citizens and others out of their money. Most of these seniors can ill afford to fall prey to these unscrupulous scammers. Yet the deals sound so easy and lucrative. It is very tempting to put out a little money for the chance of earning big returns. There are claims that 98% of those so-called deals are scams. People are trying to bully their way into the bank account of unsuspecting victims.

Senior citizens who take a job at Wal Mart as a greeter or at McDonald's to sweep up floors and clean tables might enjoy getting out of the house and seeing people. However, such a job could be cause for being bullied by people who make fun of them or ridicule them. This may come mainly from children or teenagers who are sometimes very mean and rude if not taught otherwise.

There are occasionally news stories about a senior citizen being abused and treated poorly in nursing homes, rehabilitation centers, and assisted living complexes. This could be from a staff member at the facility, but people can also be coerced into signing documents and turning over possessions and property to an unscrupulous individual or relative. These are forms of bullying.

Another problem is with seniors bullying each other in such facilities. Older people can be cruel just as children sometimes are. When someone walks into a lunchroom or activity area, others might sneer and whisper. They may be shunned as they try to find a seat for meals. An older person might be bullied by his or her peers.

Dementia in its varying degrees may cause people to be bullied or to become bullies themselves. As the mind decreases in capacity to reason and remember, someone might become aggressive and abusive to those around him. His or her frustration at not remembering might take a toll. It is an unfortunate matter, which can cause pain, but the person with the problem is not at fault.

The people who do work with the elderly as staff members of such facilities, which cater to elderly patients or residents, are to be commended for the work they do. It is not easy caring for the sick and infirm or the elderly. Some may become bullies, but most are caring individuals who do a hard job. Nurses and other medical personnel, social workers, and other staff and volunteers in retirement homes realize that there is a problem of bullying among senior citizens.

Some older people in their seventies and eighties report that they had never felt bullied as they went through their lives up to that point. They had encountered neighbors and friends whom they felt were welcoming and friendly. However, upon moving into a retirement community, people sometimes become bullying victims for the first time in their lives. There may be cliques among the older people in such communities where people are indifferent or do not accept newcomers. Just as teenage girls are often thought to be mean, seniors can also treat people unkindly whether they engaged in that behavior while they were young or not.

Older people who act like bullies may do it for the same reasons as children and young adults do. They may feel insecure or they may respond unkindly to something someone else did or said. Some people who are bullied end up being isolated either because they know they are not welcome or they stay away from others to avoid the bullying tactics. Finding a friend among such people may be difficult, but having a friend could help.

As more people grow older and the retirement communities and assisted living facilities become more populated, bullying in such places is a problem that will continue and must be addressed. Too many people are suffering from the ill effects of bullying. They need to know their limitations and what is expected of them, just as should be taught to children in schools. Those in authority may need to reach out and certainly should listen to and address any complaints from people who say they are being mistreated and bullied. Codes of conduct and rules need to be established and enforced in order to keep peace and help people be protected. Civil rights may be an issue here also.

Many seniors who are being bullied in some manner are reluctant to step up and say anything. They don't want to confront the other person because there may be retaliation. They do not want to report it to people in charge because they realize that they may have no choice but to stay in those living conditions so they don't want to make matters worse. They may just retreat and avoid people as much as possible.

Bullying is absolutely never a good thing whether it is done to a young person or an older person. It definitely harms the person being bullied, but it can destroy many aspects of life for the person who is a bully. He could be prosecuted and put in prison or his reputation could be ruined for some senseless act of bullying. He cannot feel good about himself if he is engaging in such behavior.

Chapter 9

Japanese Americans Faced Extreme Bullying

The Constitution of the United States of America should be protecting innocent citizens and legal residents of this country. There have been times when it did not. Japanese Americans faced the ultimate case of bullying by the Government when they were unjustly faced with mass racial profiling during World War II and persecuted.

Even before the Imperial Navy of Japan bombed Pearl Harbor in Hawaii on December 7, 1941, Americans of Japanese ancestry faced much discrimination and prejudice. By that time two thirds of those of Japanese heritage living in the United States were American citizens. They were the second and third generation of Japanese descent living in America. They had been born in the United States.

Japanese immigrants started arriving in the United States during the late 1800's with larger numbers coming in the early part of the 1900's. Most of the earliest immigrants were young, single men. They arrived on these shores largely for economic reasons as America was seen as the land of opportunity, and they were often recruited as laborers. Many of the men married women from Japan (some of whom were so-called "picture brides"). These new immigrants did not find a warm welcome waiting for them in what was to become their new home. Most probably expected it to be temporary until they were able to earn and save enough money to return to Japan and live comfortably. That never happened and was not an option for most of these immigrants.

As the Japanese people in the United States began to establish families, farms, and small businesses with a limited measure of success, they were often looked upon as a threat by the general population. Having distinctly different physical characteristics from European Americans and immigrants from that side of the ocean, they found themselves treated with disdain, distrust, discrimination, and outright racism. By 1925, there had been a ban placed on further immigration from Japan.

Education was stressed by the immigrant parents so a fair number of Japanese Americans had graduated from college before the 1940's. They had a difficult time securing meaningful employment in their fields of study, however, because of the discrimination and prejudice they faced. No one wanted to hire them. The doctors and lawyers often could only find patients and clients from within the Japanese American and immigrant community. They were treated unfairly by most of the general public.

Young leaders within the Japanese American community started a national organization, the Japanese American Citizens League (JACL), in 1929 to advocate for civil rights for themselves and their parents. They tried to combat the social injustice they faced.

Immediately after the bombing of Pearl Harbor, many leaders of Japanese heritage were arrested and imprisoned. They were suspected of espionage and were taken from their families, often without their families having any knowledge of where they had been taken. They lived in fear and apprehension, as did the rest of the Japanese Americans and immigrants in the United States.

Then President Franklin D. Roosevelt signed Executive Order 9066 on February 19, 1942. This gave the military commander the right to remove any persons from certain designated areas. It could have been used against others, but the Order was only enacted upon the people who were of Japanese heritage. People who were ethnically Japanese were forcibly removed from their West Coast homes with little notice, placed in temporary assembly centers, and then were incarcerated in hastily constructed camps in remote and desolate areas of the country.

The people of Japanese heritage had been suffering from the effects of prejudice and discrimination, a form of bullying, for a long time before the events of December 7, 1941, occurred. They were innocent people who faced this ultimate case of bullying and mass racial profiling by their government as they lost their freedom and nearly everything else that they possessed.

This forced and unwarranted incarceration caused huge problems for the 120,000 American citizens and immigrants who were affected by the order. Many suffered the ill effects of incarceration throughout their entire lives. Some people became ill and died in the camps. There were some who committed suicide because of the mistreatment and depression they suffered. It is hard to believe that such a thing could and did happen in the United States of America to its own citizens and legal resident alien immigrants. The causes of such actions were later determined to be racial prejudice and hatred, war hysteria, and a lack of competent political leadership in the government ranks.

The Western Defense Command under the direction of Lieutenant General John DeWitt implemented the order against the ethnic Japanese people living in the mainland West Coast states. It was clearly racist as it was used only against those who were of Japanese ancestry although it could have been used against Germans and Italians as well.

When Lieutenant General Delos Emmons, commanding general in Hawaii (which was then a United States territory), determined that it was not necessary to implement the order in the Islands, the Japanese Americans living in Hawaii were largely spared from the same treatment. He stated that anyone of Japanese descent who was considered to be a threat to the national security had already been incarcerated. It would not have been feasible in Hawaii because the Japanese people made up such a large part of the population and were important to the economy. There were estimated to be 150,000 persons of Japanese ancestry residing in Hawaii at that time.

Most of those who were directly affected by the executive order were incarcerated in the American concentration camps for the duration of the war. The basic freedoms which should be guaranteed by the Constitution to all citizens were stripped away. They were imprisoned in the barbed wire enclosures in bleak and isolated regions of the country through no fault of their own and only because of their heritage. There was no due process. They were watched over by armed guards although there was virtually nowhere to which they could escape if they had tried. People who were of Japanese ancestry and living in other parts of the country away from the West Coast were not directly and personally impacted by the order, but they suffered hardships as well because they were also viewed as the enemy. They regularly endured bullying tactics against them.

There were some of the Japanese people who protested the mistreatment or bullying by the government. They tried to resist and fight against the unjust actions placed upon them. Their protestations and objections were in vain. They were either sent to a regular prison or to another camp that was considered as a place for troublemakers. There was no recourse against the extreme bullying they suffered, but they tried to make their feelings known.

Many decades later, people were finally starting to talk about their incarceration experiences when a commission was formed to study the matter. There were people who said they wished they had at that time had the courage to fight against the unfair bullying which was showered upon them.

In the 1970's the Japanese American Citizens League (JACL) and other community organizations started a push to seek redress and reparations for those who were unfairly bullied by their government during World War II. A commission was established to study the issue, and then Congress voted to allow redress. The bill was signed by President Ronald Reagan to allow those Japanese Americans who were still living when the bill was signed to receive some redress and a formal apology from the government. They received a letter from the President of the United States. For most who received the redress, the letter was signed by President George H. W. Bush.

Conclusions of the commission found that the reasons for that gross travesty of justice were: racism, war hysteria, and a lack of competent government leadership. It was finally acknowledged that the incarceration of innocent Japanese Americans was unconstitutional and unjust. This was the goal of the redress movement to acknowledge that the incarceration was an injustice and to ensure that such an action would never be repeated against anyone else.

Although most of the general public who are aware of the unwarranted incarceration of Japanese Americans during World War II consider it a huge injustice, there are some who do not. There are people who have been advocating that the same treatment be done to American Muslims and others who may have similar appearances and characterizations to the terrorists of 9-11 and beyond. Others have suggested that undocumented immigrants be incarcerated in like manner. Innocent people should not be subjected to such treatment by the government and their fellow citizens. The unjust mass incarceration of Japanese Americans was an unfortunate episode in American history which should not have occurred. There was no due process and no justice in the matter. Such a thing definitely should never be repeated. It was clearly the intense bullying of innocent persons.

Japanese Americans want this part of American history to be better known so that no one else will ever have to suffer such injustice as when the United States Government and its leaders resorted to this extreme form of bullying against innocent persons.

Sometimes bullying tactics and conduct cannot be curtailed, but people need to try and help to be the solution to this horrible problem and mistreatment of innocent people.

Chapter 10

Sales People Can Be Bullies

Woulda, coulda, shoulda. Would have, could have, should have. Those words of regret apply all too often in the lives of many people when they have had an experience of being basically bullied into buying something they did not need or want at a time when they should have said no.

One of the worst cases of sales people using bullying tactics likely involves those who are selling used or new cars. Buying or leasing a car can become one of those times of regret if a person is not careful. After a lease or purchase agreement is signed, the buyer or lessee will have to live with it. If someone is unable to stand his/her ground and not give in to their persistent maneuvering to alter the desire and plans of the customer, it may later become a matter of regret and thinking about what *would have, could have, or should have* been done.

Before entering a dealership, it is a good idea to make some decisions. If this is not done, it becomes too easy and likely to succumb to the high pressure sales tactics that will be encountered there. Car sales people have a bad reputation and are often seen as dishonest and untrustworthy. Of course, there are good, honest, and ethical sales people out there (and they would all like to have the customers think they fit that category whether they do or not).

Pushy sales persons can often get people to buy or lease a car even if they were just looking with no intention to purchase when entering the showroom. They try to make the customer think they are providing a good deal and doing the person a huge favor. They may badger him and insist that he NEEDS to act today for his own good. They will not take no for an answer, and they keep the pressure on even if the customer tries to leave.

They will bring in reinforcements, presumably the sales manager who is authorized to give an even better deal. They may become obnoxious and rude as they try to manipulate thinking and concerns. They will likely use unscrupulous methods to get the customer in their grip. It can be considered as a form of bullying when they insist and persist relentlessly.

A couple went to visit a dealership three months before their lease on their current car was up. They wanted to get some ideas about what type of car they should get next. They definitely had not planned to lease a new car the day they visited the new car showroom.

The woman who waited on them seemed very nice. They later described her as a wolf in sheep's clothing or a witch in disguise. She was extremely friendly as she told the would-be customers about her personal life and how she had recently moved to the area with her boyfriend. She acted very interested in and concerned for the couple as they looked at new cars.

After enduring some time of extremely high pressure salesmanship, the wife suggested that they needed to go out to lunch and think about it. The sales lady then ordered lunch for them. She basically was not going to let them leave without signing papers to buy a new car. She did not want them to exit the building. She knew that they would likely never come back if she let them out of her sight. She was determined to make the sale. She offered to have their remaining payments paid on the older car until the lease was up. She tried everything she could to get them to sign papers for a new car.

The husband liked the new car that they were considering and became convinced that it was a good deal that she was proposing. His wife tried to resist, but she eventually let herself give in to the high pressure tactics. Every excuse to wait was shot down with some perceived solution being proposed. They later realized that they had actually been bullied into taking an action that the wife at least had not wanted to do at that time. There was no recourse after they left the dealership with papers signed and an extra car for three months that they certainly did not need. It turned out that there were some additional costs involved.

If a person does not want to be bullied into a decision that is unplanned and unwanted which might cause regret, it is important not to give in to the tactics used for coercion. Keeping a firm upper hand and resolve can help someone to not become a customer and victim when that is not what is desired. It is important to be strong enough to just say no. It is wise to use the same admonishment to young people when faced with the temptation to use drugs and alcohol, and JUST SAY NO.

Car sales people are trained to make the sale the first time they are visited by a prospective customer. If they don't get a sale on the initial contact, they most likely will not have a chance with the people again. They know that when someone leaves their showroom, it is extremely doubtful the person would ever return.

If some checking and thinking about their "deal" is carefully done, it may be discovered that it is not that good. Shopping around might prove a better option, but it takes a strong will to resist the next sales person encountered. The people who sell cars try very hard to not allow the prospective buyer to leave without buying.

A purchase or lease of an automobile is a major event. It is the biggest or next biggest (for those who own a home) expenditure for most people. It is something that should be considered and looked at carefully before signing any papers. Sales people do not want the consumer to do any checking or thinking. They want to get you when you are vulnerable, and they will wear you down until you are just that.

There are certain ideas that could be used to avoid problems of bullying down the road. Discussing the matter thoroughly even before going to a dealership will help. Options can be considered and decided ahead of time, in order to not be coerced into making a purchase that day if that is not the intention. Pushy sales people can get their fangs into would-be customers, and they work very hard to wear people down. It is important to not admit that a purchase could be made that day and may be a consideration. Sticking to the plans as made beforehand can help to fight off the possibly bullying tactics that could come into play.

It is a good idea to develop the ability to just say no to pushy, aggressive, high pressured sales people. Make them take no for an answer until the time is right for a car purchase. Don't let them high pressure you and bully you into something you don't want to do. You will be happier with your eventual purchase and have fewer regrets. They should not have control over their potential customers. People should have their freedom and rights.

Although some dealerships may advertise that a car could be returned within seven days if the buyers have regrets about their purchase, that is not customary. It is usually too late after the papers are signed and the car is driven off the lot.

Another category of sales people who may use bullying tactics is the stockbroker. They try to pressure people to make investments they do not want to make and place money where they do not choose to put it.

Home repair people who come to the home for a specific purpose may actually become relentless sales persons as they try to convince the homeowner to buy additional repairs and services that may not be necessary.

Many people are looking for extra income by checking into online home based business opportunities. These industries may include numerous people who are selling their wares. They use bullying tactics to convince people to buy their products. People who get on lists are very often inundated with sales material they do not want. The perpetrators of these programs are trying to wear them down and convince them to make a purchase. They may make false promises and claims that could be considered as a bullying tactic to rein in unsuspecting victims.

All sales people are not bullies and do not use those tactics, of course, but there are a fair number who do. A firm resolve to not give in to the bullies is necessary for peace of mind and possibly for the sake of a person's well being economically and mentally.

Chapter 11

The Tragedy of Suicide From Bullying

It is a sad situation when bullying has been allowed to escalate to the point of causing a person to want to end it all and to attempt to escape the bullying by committing suicide. Too many lives are wasted from the pointless acts of bullying. Young people should not have to feel intimidated and persecuted so much that they become so unhappy from the unkind acts perpetrated against them that they feel there is no recourse but to end their lives. It is a tragedy, which occasionally and all too often, occurs from bullying.

Some studies indicate that a third of children in schools report that they have been bullied. Bullying seems to be more prevalent now than in days gone by partly because people are more aware that it is happening. Perhaps the bullies are feeling more confident that they can do mean things to others without incurring any consequences.

There has been shown to be a strong correlation between bullying and suicide. Studies indicate that suicide among young people takes over 4,000 lives per year. These are people who were otherwise healthy and should not have had their lives cut short during the tender years of youth.

Bullying is a serious problem in society. Too often it leads to negative results after a person has been bullied to the point of desperation. Their health may suffer, but suicide should not be an option. It could be prevented if more people would be willing to reach out and help.

There are often warning signs that a person may be contemplating suicide. Parents, teachers, and friends can be on the lookout for these signals if a person appears to be especially unhappy and despondent. They may talk about death, dying, and suicide or may be asking questions about death. They might give away prized possessions with which they would not normally want to part. They may say goodbye as if it is final and the last time. Simply acting depressed and dejected may be a clue that there are underlying problems. They may keep to themselves and not show an interest in other people or the things going on around them. They may suddenly be intent on participating in potentially dangerous activities such as skydiving or scuba diving. They could talk to people and tell them that life is too hard.

Everyone will have problems, some very serious, at various times throughout their lives. No one can escape this life without trials and difficulties. It is hard to tell if an ordeal is so severe that it could cause them to consider the ultimate and final act of suicide. Talking to them and trying to get them to tell their true feelings may be the only way to know what they are thinking and contemplating. If it seems serious enough, professional help may be advisable and necessary.

People often suffer in silence because they feel desperate and may not think that people care what happens to them. They may feel that their family and friends would be better off without them. They could feel guilt for making other people miserable. The warning signs should be heeded if they are noticed. Many suicides could have been prevented if someone recognized the signs and cries for help before it was too late.

If and when a person realizes that someone else, particularly a young person, is behaving or speaking in the manner of a suicidal individual, it is a good idea to intervene. It can and should start with honest communication. Showing a genuine interest in the person should help and might curtail the despair and the hopeless act that is being contemplated.

Adults, such as parents and teachers, and peers, such as friends and fellow students, would do well to be more cognizant of what is going on with children and teenagers. If their normal behavior changes drastically, there is likely to be a problem such as being bullied. The victims of bullying are usually reluctant to bring up the subject, but they may be anxious to tell someone if only another person asked questions and showed enough interest in them.

Many young people feel alone and do not confide in their parents regularly. They need to be drawn out to talk about any problems that they may be experiencing. It is the duty and responsibility of parents to be aware of what is going on in their children's lives. It is not an easy thing to do. Although they may be unwilling to tell their parents about their problems, perhaps another trusted individual could be enlisted to assist such as a teacher, counselor, coach, or church leader.

The problem causing children to be bullied may be their home situation. Maybe they are being made fun of and called names because they do not have a traditional family or their family has noticeable problems such as economic stress or poverty. They may not want to tell their parents about the problems, which could seemingly place blame on the parents. They may hide their true feelings and concerns. This could be damaging to them.

People, young or old, who are thinking about suicide should talk to someone before the problems become worse. They need to resolve the issues before they become so bad that suicide seems to be the only way out. There are services where people can make an anonymous phone call to talk to a stranger about their problems. This is preferred by some instead of telling someone they know about the trials and hardship they are experiencing. The person on the other end of the line will have been trained to offer assistance and guidance in such situations. They provide a listening ear.

If parents find out that their child is being bullied at school, it is important to inform the proper authorities right away so that the bullying can be stopped before the harmful effects become more pronounced. It needs to be ended before the consequences cause serious danger and repercussions to the bullied person and possibly to the bully as well.

The National Institute of Health has reported that suicide has been the third leading cause of death for young people ages 15 to 24. Young men ages 20-24 have the second highest rate for suicide with the highest rate being older men over the age of 65. The older generation may be at risk for suicide because of declining physical and mental health, which makes them feel useless and ready to end it all. The younger generation is quite likely to commit suicide because of depression and anxiety caused from problems stemming from such acts as bullying.

Although men are more likely to attempt and succeed at suicide, it is also becoming a major problem among young teenage girls who may be the victims of cyber bullying which occurs when unkind and usually untrue posts are made about them online. Bullies think they can anonymously post photos and untrue or harmful words about another person to ridicule them. It becomes difficult for the victims of such unfair tactics to face others and to attend school where people snicker and whisper about them. These young girls are often suffering in silence until they feel they can endure it no longer so that taking their own life seems the only or best option. That is a sad commentary on what can happen when bullying takes place.

Often those who commit suicide did talk about it to friends or parents, but they were not taken seriously. No one really believed it would happen. After someone does commit that final act with what they probably consider to be successful results, people close to the person often recall that there were warning signs. They did not recognize them at the time. The person could have been calling out for help, but people around him or her did not do anything to help because they did not think it was a real threat.

Parents, friends, and relatives of people who do commit suicide may need counseling themselves to deal with the tragedy. They may feel undue and undeserved guilt and shame. They might have been able to prevent it, but the results may have been the same. They need to talk about it so that they will not become victims themselves. They must realize that they may have missed signals, but it is quite likely that they could not have prevented it. They need to deal with it so that they can have peace.

Suicide is the tragic, ultimate, and final result from bullying. It is something that hurts the person who leaves this world to find relief. It causes pain and suffering for the family and friends left behind. It can cause extreme problems for the person who engaged in the bullying against an innocent person. The bully may suffer huge consequences as well if prosecution is a result of the bullying actions. Undoubtedly, the bully should and will experience guilt at causing the unfortunate suicide. It affects and brings harm to many people.

Chapter 12

Helping Others Who May Be Bullied

People who are being bullied usually need help in dealing with the bully. It is often difficult for the person to stop the bullying without some outside intervention. The victims may not ask for help and may be afraid to tell other people that they are being bullied. They fear repercussions from the bully. They may even want to avoid getting the other person in trouble. They may think that no one will believe them or care. It behooves others to be aware and look for problems when depression and despondency are noticed in a friend, family member, or associate.

While some people who are bullied may feel strong enough to stand up to the bully and possibly retaliate against them, such actions could cause further problems. Being aggressive against a bully is not a good idea. Sometimes a bigger or more powerful friend or possibly an authority figure may step in and respond to the bully on behalf of the victim. That may cause the bully to become intimidated himself and to retreat.

A television show depicted actors portraying bullying and unkind acts against other people. These were enacted with unknowing and unsuspecting individuals as bystanders and observers in public places such as restaurants, in meetings, or on the street. The reactions of people who watched the perpetrators of the unkindness and rudeness were recorded. Some people stepped in to help, but most were reluctant to intervene or interfere, possibly for fear of getting involved. It takes courage to stick up for another person, particularly a stranger who is being bullied. It shows a remarkable sense of justice for someone to stand up and help someone they do not even know.

Parents and teachers can help children to avoid being bullied or becoming a bully by proper education and training. Children should be taught to respect others and their differences. They should be made to realize that there will always be people who are different from them. They must be taught be tolerant and kind in their dealings with other people. They should be taught that bullying and violence should never be an option. They need to realize that they are all just people with feelings and concerns.

Children should be taught various methods to deal with bullies if the need arises. They should watch out for themselves and others. They should be aware of their surroundings and pay attention to other people. They should avoid people who appear to be a threat to their well being. They could change the route they normally take to and from school to avoid the bully. They should walk away when confronted with bullying and not get into a heated confrontation with the bully. Trying to ignore the bully and the mean things being said is not always easy, but it may be necessary to avoid further problems. They should not show that the words are upsetting and hurtful to them.

It is important for children to be taught that they are people of great worth. They should be confident enough in their own self-esteem that they do not need to believe the words being tossed their way by a bully. They need to learn that they are not at fault if they have done nothing wrong.

Children need to feel confident that it is okay to ask for help. A parent, teacher, friend, or leader should be told about the bullying problem so that it may be eliminated. They need to be taught to help and respect each other. If they see someone getting bullied, they should reach out and try to assist. The best way is likely to tell someone else about it. The person being bullied may not want to tell, but another party should be able to inform the proper people in charge, such as teachers, leaders, and law enforcement officers. If someone were bullying them, they would probably appreciate a friend or observer to intervene to stop the harassment and mistreatment. They should be willing to help each other.

Showing respect for everyone no matter their circumstances is a way to stop bullying. Bullies do not show respect to others. Children need to be taught to respect others in order for them to avoid becoming bullies and to help those who may be bullied.

The fact that smart phones are equipped with video cameras makes documenting bullying behavior a fairly easy matter. Most people, from small children to senior citizens, own a cell phone. Bad behavior such as all types of bullying can be recorded and shown to the proper authorities in order to put a stop to the negative behavior of bullying.

There are also the suggestions to be kind to the bully and try to be civil to him or her. That is not usually an easy route to take, and the bully is unlikely to reciprocate with kindness. It may be worth a try. Some people have tried giving cookies or a candy bar to a bully in an effort to curtail the bad behavior. It could work.

It may be helpful to develop an action plan for children in case they are confronted with the problem of being bullied. They should be aware of what bullying behavior is and how they can react to it. They should feel safe to tell someone about the problem so that it can be stopped before bad consequences occur.

Parents should create an atmosphere in the home where bullying behavior is not acceptable. Children should be kind to their siblings. It is not an easy matter to control the behavior of children as they are prone to act out and react to various situations. Fighting is all too common among families, but some parents have managed to control the behavior of their children to avoid physical confrontations and verbal abuse. It is a worthwhile goal to create an atmosphere of love and respect in the home. It is effective to boost the self-respect and self-esteem of children. Children should try to get along with their family members. Then the children will not be likely to become bullies, and they can be taught what to do if a situation arises where they are bullied by others.

Being bullied creates bad feelings and hardship. Many people, from kids to teens and adults, are bullied in their life times. Sometimes when bullying is taken too far, people take their own lives to put an end to it. Bullies may think they are having fun by tormenting innocent individuals whom they know or do not know.

Education is the key. Being educated about the effects of bullying and the behaviors of bullies and their victims must be encouraged and achieved in order to combat the problem and to help others.

Bullies are a pain as well as being mean and scary. The victims of bullies need to be made to feel that it is not their fault that they are being bullied. They are not alone, and they should seek help. Bullying can be dangerous, but victims can get help.

It is difficult to change anyone's behavior unless the person wants to change. However, if they are motivated enough by learning and possibly kindness shown to them, they may want to change their behavior.

It is vital that people learn to deal with bullies for the sake of the victims especially but also for the sake of the bully. If the bully does not deal with his actions by correcting them, he could become worse and end up in prison after his actions have escalated into more violent or destructive behavior.

There are a number of government and social agencies that can help people to deal with bullying when it is something that the person and family cannot handle. It is possible to find help before problems become worse. Matters of concern should come to the forefront so that people can deal with them effectively. Hiding problems and failure to share issues with responsible parties can lead to bad outcomes. Help is available and should be utilized when necessary.

Bullying should not be tolerated because it destroys too many lives in the process of humiliating and harassing another human being. It is a destructive practice that is ruining lives. The eradication of bullying is a worthwhile goal for which to work.

SUMMARY

Bullying will likely continue to be a problem in society. It affects a lot of people on a daily basis. There is too much of bullying in the acts and behavior of too many people. It is unfortunate that there will continue to be ignorant, intolerant, unkind, and rude people who bully others in order to make themselves look better. Prejudice, racism, and discrimination are still facts of life although conditions have improved measurably in some areas over the past decades since civil rights became a major issue. Bullying should be considered as a huge problem that the general public, schools, government, churches, communities, and individuals must face and address. People should not feel unsafe and threatened in their schools and communities, in their neighborhoods, in their workplaces, and in their daily activities. They should not have to live in fear because of being bullied.

People who are being bullied should not feel that they are to blame for the mistreatment they are receiving from bullies. It is not their fault. They should seek help from others who may be able to offer assistance, whether it be parents, teachers, church leaders, friends, or law enforcement officers.

Friends and family members can watch for signs that bullying is occurring. They should pay attention to what is going on in the lives of those close to them and around them. They should keep the lines of communication open. They can reach out to help and offer to tell people in authority who could assist to rectify the problems. There is a lot of help out there, but people must be willing to support others and/or to seek help.

People should be made to feel that they are valuable and of great worth so that bullying should not affect them adversely. They should have respect for themselves and others. They need to feel personal self-respect and self-esteem.

Bullying is a big concern in the daily lives of many people, both young and old. It is absolutely necessary that this problem of bullying continue to be addressed, especially by school authorities and law enforcement personnel as well as family members.

Bullying against innocent persons should not be tolerated, whether it is being perpetrated by individuals, groups, law enforcement, community and church leaders, or the government itself. People should not lose their freedom and civil rights at the hands of a bully.

No one can make it through this life without trouble of one kind or another. Bullying should not be one of those problems. It is an unnecessary evil of society that should not be tolerated.

The issue of bullying concerns everyone. People need to be more kind, compassionate, and caring in order to remedy the problem because…Bullying is not just a kids' problem. It is a matter of civil rights.

Thank you for reading this book.

Hopefully, enough people will be interested in the subject of Bullying that it can be curtailed or even eradicated.

Life is to be enjoyed. It should not be ruined by the senseless and unwarranted acts of bullies.